PATRICK CHAPMAN

a promiscuity of spines

NEW AND SELECTED POEMS

salmonpoetry

Published in 2012 by
Salmon Poetry
Cliffs of Moher, County Clare, Ireland
Website: www.salmonpoetry.com
Email: info@salmonpoetry.com

Copyright © Patrick Chapman, 2012

ISBN 978-1-908836-14-4

All rights reserved. No part of this publication may be reproduced or transmitted in any form or by any means, electronic or mechanical, including photography, recording, or any information storage or retrieval system, without permission in writing from the publisher. The book is sold subject to the condition that it shall not, by way of trade or otherwise, be lent, resold or otherwise circulated without the publisher's prior consent in any form of binding or cover other than that in which it is published and without a similar condition, including this condition, being imposed on the subsequent purchaser.

Cover design and art direction: *Vaughan Oliver at v23*
Photography: *Marc Atkins at panoptika.net*

Salmon Poetry receives financial support from The Arts Council

For Sara

Acknowledgements

This volume presents a selection from my poetry books written between 1987 and 2010, as well as a collection of new work. Grateful acknowledgements to the editors of the following, where most of the new poems, some in earlier drafts, were first published or broadcast, or are forthcoming.

Ireland: *Burning Bush 2*, nos. 1 and 4; *Census 3*; *Crannóg 30*; *Cyphers 73*; *Over the Edge* blog; *Rhyme & Reason* (Dublin South FM); *The Stinging Fly*, vol. 2, issues 19 and 22; *Windows 20*.

U.S.: *About Place Journal*, vol. I, issue III; *BlazeVOX12 – Spring 2012*; *Gargoyle #60*; *Naugatuck River Review*, issue 7; *Prairie Schooner*, vol. 85, no. 4; *The Raintown Review*, vol. 10, issue 1 and vol. 11, issue 1.

The Oonagh Young Gallery commissioned 'Background Radiation' for its exhibition, *Timecoloured Place* (Sept. 10 to Oct. 29, 2011).

Contents

from *JAZZTOWN* (1991)

Love	13
Cities	14
As Seen From the Lake	15
Swimming	16
Jazztown	17
Worm	18
Worms	19
Drowned Spacecraft	20
Sentient Glass	21
The Walls Replied	22
Blissed Out	23
Burnout	24
Home	25
Acid Head Movie Show	26
Night Landing	27
Inhale	28

from *THE NEW PORNOGRAPHY* (1996)

Night on 109th Street	31
An Eye in Central Park	32
San Andreas Fault	33
A Dream of Space Flight	34
Nantahala Falls	35
Extraterrestrials	36
The Communist	37
Backward Child	38
Jocasta Tree	40
Vibrating Love Nest	41
Viral	42
Sub Rosa	43
Robert Mapplethorpe: Aspects of *Self Portrait 1988*	44

from *BREAKING HEARTS AND TRAFFIC LIGHTS* (2007)

Tiergarten Trilogy	47
Summer of Love, Vol. 1	49
First Christmas by the Sea	50
Touchpaper Star	51
Cobain	52
Banns	53
Hope of Ray	54
Easter Comet	55
I Loved You Here	56
Windows on the World	58
Post-Mortem	59
Mercy Fuck	60
Covetous Foetus	61
Rain	62
Moon Sea Time	64
Spiders	65
Sea of Tranquillity	66
Music Downstairs	67
Eidolon	68
Cicatrice	69
Tunisia, Winter 1998	70

from *A SHOPPING MALL ON MARS* (2008)

Empire Diner	73
Nostalgia	74
Skydiving Narcissus	76
Turing's Apple	77
Glossolalia	78
Style Goddess	79
A Shopping Mall on Mars	80
Inversion Ward	81
Drown	82
Wave Collapse	83
Descent	84
To a House of Tin and Timber	85
The Philosopher Dances	86

from *THE DARWIN VAMPIRES* (2010)

The Darwin Vampires	89
La Femme Éperdue	90
The Mourning Doves	91
Husk	92
Love Watches for Death	94
Baby	96
Skywalker Country	97
Saint Dracula	98
Crush	99
Junky	100
Freakchild	101
The Golden Age of Aviation	102
4°	104
4'33"	105
Reflecting Angel	106
You Murder the Sun	107
Hidradenitis Suppurativa	110
Anaphylaxis	111
Manila Hemp	112
The Forest	113
Gloria Mundi	114

A PROMISCUITY OF SPINES

Volcano Day	117
A Promiscuity of Spines	118
Visitor	120
Sleight	121
Timing	122
Glue	123
The Lion and the Boy	124
Winter	125
Shokushu Goukan	126
Selas	127
Black Smoke	128

The Boudoir Grand	129
The Jerusalem Syndrome	130
Giddy Andromeda	131
Brittle Hour	132
Cut	133
The Orphan	134
Apollo	136
The National Style 'O' Resonator	137
The Celluloid Angel	138
Dragonfly	140
Days	141
The Idlewild Rose	142
Ouse	144
Tiberian	145
The *Voyager* Mote	146
Background Radiation	148
Acheron	150
The Amnesia-to-Melancholy Ratio	152
Doppelgänger Clues	153

from

Jazztown

(1991)

Love

Later, my floorboards covered other lovers,
But I couldn't cover you in there.
Instead, I took you in my arms
And put your pieces in a bag.

Then I cleaned the flat.

I tucked you underneath my bed:
The closest you had ever been
To sleeping with me.

One day your scent came, filled the room.
It told me that the worst of love
Is letting go.
That night, although you smelled of fear,
I put you out into the street.

Since then, I see you everywhere.

I find you in my headphones
When I listen to the symphony
That used to terrify you.
The silence between movements is like you,
Holding your breath.

Cities

I watch you stretch
limbs like a city
in the bathroom mirror:
the archways of your knees
and the aqueducts above
like London Bridge,
opening to strangers.

Those summer visitors
demanded in a foreign tongue
the relics that you would not give;
they took the city with them when they left.

I see you now,
sacked in skies of glass:
the Thames has burst its banks
and is howling in the doorways.

As Seen From the Lake

Toronto has its cranes in me;
Tonight it's taken me
From Tweedsmuir Avenue to Harbourfront.
Beneath a bridge I face the lake
That separates me from New York,
Niagara and Buffalo,
These places far removed from Boyle.

The distance smells of Hamilton
But I can not inhale that far;
I turn and walk towards Yonge Street
Where the whores outside the skin shows
Down past Sam the Record Man
Are waiting for this city
To collapse inside their bodies.

Swimming

Mrs Malenky and Mr Kaminsky
Went into the ocean together,
Still wearing their regulation overalls.

Once in the ocean,
They joined up, unseen,
Squirming out of their overalls,
Taking in brine,
Linking arms, linking legs,
As they bobbed up and down
Like a pair of pink bubbles.

Love me, said Mrs Malenky.
Love me, said Mr Kaminsky.
Take us, they said to the ocean.
Take us to America.

Jazztown

Einar and Mo in their bed
Know little or nothing of Jazz,
But they have a tape made of brass:
Music for the Knee Plays.
Einar is living in the future
And Mo is counting things,
Which is fine as long as the summer lasts.
But what will they do then?

They will listen to the city like a double bass,
Hear the crickets in the walls make drums,
And beyond, hear the neighbours argue like trumpets.
When they go out, there's the sun like a saxophone.
They will skate on the lake, their blades like hi-hats
Against a backdrop of trees stripped bare like a tune.

Worm

While the cornerstone of agriculture reads my palm,
Moving across my life line very slowly,
It will not properly differentiate between me and a field
Until it tries to plough me.

Of course, what I remember of oligochaetic annelids
I remember from biology lessons that insisted:
    – that a worm reproduces passionlessly
    – that it is boneless and eyeless and toothless
    – that it finds clay palatable.

Round the heel of my hand, the worm suggests
    thousands of worms,
Thousands engulfing my arm, like the circuits of a brain
That has burst through the skull and has discovered
    Independence of the body.

Moving under my sleeve, the worm finds a darkness
That is warmer than the earth in winter, but less malleable.

Worms

Worms come to me in my sleep.
Once I had visions of a race of nuclear-accident victims
Living in boisterous harmony under the ground
Between the bombed-out stations
Of Tottenham Court Road and Oxford Circus.
Now it is the worms, masses of them.
They have replaced the trains
As the most reliable form of public transport.
A million worms can lift a body all the way to Covent Garden.

The underground itself reeks of the worms.
Each station is a terminus between segments,
Each line a different worm, overlapping;
Slick bodies ruling beautiful London.
It is at this point in my dream that I wake up:
Stranded between stations, holding onto the cables
To avoid falling onto the line,
I am pressed close to the wall as an express gestalt of worms
Snowballs towards me, and I forget which segment I am in.

Drowned Spacecraft

Her silver body slipped
Below the silk dark of the Mississippi,
Drowning her by fire
Until she fell into the arms of silt.
This landing was unplanned:
On board, a New Year party
Interrupted in the middle of a slow set.
Dinner-suited gentlemen
And ladies wearing feather boas
Relived the Roaring Twenties
In a ballroom big enough for water.
Then the fire started;
Seemed as though the sun
Had dipped behind Manhattan
And had risen once again
On board the ship.

Sentient Glass

I imagined that someone
Had invented sentient glass
And that we had rubbed our bodies
Up against your nightlit window.
This glass could deduce
From the very touch of our skin
How long our colons were
And how many milligrammes of bile
Spilled in the half hour
After a typical light snack
Into our swooning duodena.

It could analyse these things
And give a condensation readout
On its surface
But it could not analyse intangibles like:
We have shared each other with the glass
And we are hungry once again.

The glass would watch us eat
As, forks in hand, we would contemplate
Conditions on another planet
Where the time it takes for us to eat,
On this world,
Could be the time it takes on that world
For a pane of sentient glass to go senile.

The Walls Replied

For days you wouldn't sleep without
A drink to draw your eyelids down.
Your blankets were too difficult,
Your bed too temperamental.
And you outstared the sun or moon
Or kissed the walls and called their names,
Names burned into the pillowcase
And only you could know them.
Insisting that the walls replied,
Your fingers stroked your eyelids down;
The walls replied and called your name.

Blissed Out

Before this building is completed
We will walk in the foundations
Under the influence of alcohol
And wonder where the bedroom will be.

Where will be the living room,
The kitchen and reception? And then
Where will we make children
And, having made them,
Where will we put them?

We will place our hands into the breezeblocks,
Wondering what rats will live there
And what ghosts, in years to come,
Will drag the past up from behind the plaster,

Where the wiring and the pipes will hang,
Will constitute this building's nerves.
Having contemplated these things,
We will find the still-wet concrete in the hall
And make ourselves, in footprints, into history.

Burnout

The firemen found
two jellied children
in the ground floor bedroom,
clinging to each other
as though freezing –
Siamese twins in death.

Walls had echoed
the cacophonies of flame
through which the parents had escaped.
The upstairs windows, smashed,
had let them live,
like ghosts already.

Home

Their faces are the maps of their country
Their bodies
are occupied territory

She remembers the chill
of his breath on her back
like a chemical weapon
delivered in the darkness

that spawned their bundle of joy

It
babbles nursery rhymes
as it stares through the bars
of its pen

Acid Head Movie Show

The acid head movie show opened today.
He saw it at three, in monochrome.

It was a film in which his father
Slashed a grocer with a breadknife
And his mother whipped her only son
With stripped bare curtain wire
Making troughs of blood so deep,
You'd grow a garden in his back.

The credits rolled and he threw up
Into the lap of the girl beside him.
He suspected she identified with mother.

Then, taking his nostalgia home
And weeping open to the world,
He trashed the television set.

Night Landing

In her nightdress is the pattern of a ghost.
There are twenty-and-a-half small spirits sewn into the nylon.
The child steps into the landing
To the sound of music from below:
Hank Williams howling at the moon
While her parents try to make her brother.
The girl has seen the devil every night.
Painted on the ceiling, he has spoken to her
Through her eyes that do not know the mystery
Of streetlamps through a windowpane.
Her hands go down the banister
Till she sits on the bottom stair.
Hank Williams stops; she hears her parents crying out
Through the living room door.
She leaves the stair and quietly enters
The scene of her parents' agony
And senses her brother swimming, incomplete, between them.

Inhale

My parents are dead
but the house is a bottle for their scents.
In the room where I was made,
where the Xs and Ys coincided as though
I were a point on a graph
that could measure the strength of a smell,
I remember what they used to play
as a contrast to her cassolette:
The Correct Use Of Soap,
as they tried to retain
a full head of youth
like seed that was spilled
but was too good to waste.
Instead it is here.
It is crusted on sheets
along with remembrance of mildew,
of phlegm,
and the fragrance of lilies,
the bare hint of blood.
It is masking their pheromones,
hiding the stale smell of love.

from
The New Pornography
(1996)

Night on 109th Street

Forbidden to smoke in the apartment,
I sit up on the roof and watch the trails of passing aeroplanes
And automobile streams of red and brilliant white on Broadway.

I can hear the car alarms set off by landing firecrackers;
See the fire hydrant spray an arc across the street.

I spy on Pedro Gomez doing business on the stoop with neighbours,
Drinking muddy beer infused with cheap tabasco sauce.
Sometimes he will piss between the buildings.

By De Los Santos travel shop beside La Ronda bar,
A Mustang, live with light, pumps hot *merengue*
While the driver – buying beer in L'Español off-licence take away –
Is asking Pedro's daughter: 'Baby, how much for a suck?'

From an open third floor window comes a sudden creak of cello;
From another, further down, I hear a football game in Spanish.

A man in an adjacent building – cooking supper in the nude –
Will later masturbate into his window box nasturtiums.

In a taller building opposite a woman puts to bed a child
In front of whom, this evening, I have seen her making love.

After I have smoked enough I walk towards the stairs
And climb across the walls by which someone from down below
Found me asleep this morning, in the sunshine, getting burnt.

An Eye in Central Park

Last night, between
the Summerstage and wall,
I found an eye.

Its rods and cones inert,
the eye was caked in sand
and trailing nerve tissue.

Operational,
it might have witnessed
jogging, wilding, rollerblading,

Shakespeare in the Park
or vagabonds evicted
from Strawberry Fields.

I picked it up.
It had definitely been
a human eye.

In my hand the membrane burst
and humour greased my palm
so I put it in my pocket

wondering if the final image
captured on the retina
was of a plucking finger.

San Andreas Fault

'I live on the fault line,'
whispers Anabel into her dictaphone.

She frets that when tectonic plates
make quakes in California
and it crumbles into the Pacific –
America, distracted, will not notic
e.

A Dream of Space Flight

At the Air and Space Museum, alone,
Vacationing in Washington,
I look down from the body
Of the never-to-be-space-flown *Sky
Lab* sister ship at Sally Ride in mannequin.

Since *Columbia* first hit the sky,
My only ambition has been
To look from on high at the land
Where, in the fifties, my husband
Had built his own radio station;
To marvel a while at Long Island
Where first I had fallen in love;
To see the Earth once from above
Before I die.

Nantahala Falls

We rafted seven miles along the Nantahala river.
Often, we would pull in to a bank to bail out water.
One such time, a snake stunned Kim in fear.

I was thrown at Nantahala Falls, the final rapid.
Caught between the rubber and the rock,
I clawed above the surface then slipped back –
Ready to let water make me cork.
I clawed again and found the cord;
Michael and Orla pulled me aboard.

We landed on the bank where buses waited;
Dragged the raft ashore, upturned it;
Banged lifejackets on the gravel; chatted
About reptiles, chiggers, oars and drowning, rapids.

I sat on a rock and, shaking water from a shoe,
Recalled the anaesthetic Nantahala, coming to.

Extraterrestrials

The reflected clouds I saw from Albert Bridge
Appeared to float on the Lagan
Like boat-planes from another planet.

On the road to Dublin I passed pylons
Massed inside a compound,
Their lights remote: a star field
Through which ETs have arrived.

You find their effects in the landscape.
I took with me a shard of stained-glass window:
A fragment of the Crown bar
Made forensic by a car bomb.

The Communist

I am buying dated atlases – drawn up
Before a port wine stain became our map –
To stack them, thousands tall,
Like bricks in some new Berlin Wall.

Backward Child

Back before senses,
A knot of flesh unties,
An incision is unmade.

Waters, unbroken again, swirl.
I curl and close my eyes, an embryo.

Placenta reattached and agony annulled,
Lips press closed.

My heart rewinds,
Brain becomes ganglia.
I am a zygote.

*Elsewhere, baby clothes rewrap, unwrap again
And find themselves back in the shop.*

A speck lodged in the lining of the uterus, then loose,
I am gametes at point of contact, separating.

Suddenly, the ovum hits fallopian;
Spermatozoa hightail back to vulva
Where a penis is withdrawing.

They coalesce into a milk
That nestles back inside the testicles;
Ovum finds an ovary and sleeps.

*The woman on the bed is cooling.
Arched, she untears panties off her hips:
Her stomach muscles tight, her belly flat.*

The man is buttoning and off the boil.
He says 'I love you' in reverse
And, backwards, leaves the room.

The woman, whom he'd woken, dreams
That soon he will arrive in here
To interrupt her sleep.

When the night grows back into the day
Through evening, afternoon and morning
– This night in which I have been unconceived –
The man and woman have not even met.

Jocasta Tree

One day, the boy stood beside her
and hugged her as roughly
as twelve-year-old arms would allow.

Then he let her pierce him with a branch.

Her sap commingled with his blood until
– ecstatic with her juice in him –
he began to resemble her.

In dreams on rainy days, he grew bark breasts.
Awake, his elbows and his knees
adopted timber-carapace.

His toes became roots:
cambium-nacre probing for moisture
osmotically introduced
into his lymphatic system.

His arms became branches wrapped around her.

When the first wisps of puberty
happened to him,
she took him inside her and he died.

Vibrating Love Nest

Most nights, half an hour
after you have rolled away,
you ask if I'm all right.

I say:
'Uh-huh…'

But not tonight.

Tonight you have gone out
to drink some woman pretty;
left me to my own devices:

spotted dick
vibrating love egg
silver lady finger

Viral

Beneath the epidermis is a battered endoderm,
The flesh gone to pulp.
There is as yet no outward sign of injury.

The brain is already dissected
(Though meninges are intact):
Dura matter, arachnoid, pia matter.

This cadaver has been scooped out
But its shell, when struck,
Will register none of the hollowness.

Sub Rosa

Watching a lover wash cutlery,
One glove concealing a lesion
On a hand that sails through water
Like a submarine of flesh:
The fingers, bony periscopes
That spy in wrong directions.

Robert Mapplethorpe: Aspects of *Self-Portrait, 1988*

Shutter Open

Left hand clutching the knee,
Attempting to reclaim
The patella from infection.

Right hand clenching in a relic gesture
Reminiscent of an infant sucking its thumb.

Time Lapse

The props in this photograph
Are already transforming.

The dressing gown becomes a coffin;
The large leather armchair, a fire.
The crown-embroidered slippers walk away.

Development

Soon after this self-portrait
The world made its excuses and left,
Closing my eyelids behind it.

from
Breaking Hearts and Traffic Lights
(2007)

Tiergarten Trilogy

Trees of the Tear Garden

In the last months of war,
Starving Berliners
Would chop down for firewood
Trees that had endured
The constant bombardment.

Now, the trees are numbered.

Between lanes lit by lamp posts
From towns the world over,
The ones that survived
Stand a little taller
Than the post-war plantation.

Kaiser-Wilhelm Memorial Church

In flux on Budapesterstrasse,
Beside Kaiser-Wilhelm's
– The roof still agape –
I see through the bomb damage:
Sky of a bomber.

Black birds are perching on jags
Like the reincarnations of airmen.

Memory Safari

It is forbidden to photograph the animals.
I snap a red deer. I freeze a flamingo.

I hunt for the elephant picture
Promised to the friend
Who had lent me her camera.

As evening falls, I sit on a bench
And watch the Zoo station across from the Zoo.

The Pentax is trained to detect any sign
Of the lover I'm here to forget.

Summer of Love, Vol. 1

Their first weekend, he loaded the stereo with batteries
And tilted it on the back seat. While she drove,
They played a selection of music cassettes:
Ella Fitzgerald, Marianne Faithfull, a trove
Of golden oldie records. Melanie sings
The Rolling Stones. Mama Cass is dreaming.

She took them west in her old car
Past Edgeworthstown where she'd been born,
Through Longford where her parents ran
A guest house. On to Oughterard, for
Painted candles from De Lacy's.

How privileged he felt, to be with her,
Downing warm Guinness in Naughton's,
Counting strange sea shells washed up on the shore,
Taking the salt of the incoming air
Like seasoning on their kisses, tongues
Bunched up in their mouths like molluscs.

First Christmas by the Sea

Snow fell, layered on the house.
Inside, the two were celebrating
Six whole months of happiness.

Their Christmas goose was cooking
In the oven while they sat, undressed
– With no pretence to speak of –
In front of yuletide television:
Moira Shearer dancing. They
Admired her dress, the Technicolor.
Soon, they were embracing.

They began to flirt with
Recklessness – but paused to take
Precautions. Frame by frame,
The Red Shoes rolled.

Some time later, checking
That the weather was improving,
They had dinner, pulled a cracker.

In the small hours, after wine, warm hearth and sleep,
They woke to find the television on.
Somehow, snow had got inside the house.

Touchpaper Star

We stand back, watch the rocket rise
Too briefly in a night-sky arc.
It bursts into a globe of stars
That expands away from us,
Contracts towards the park.

In this way, we create dimension.

'Light the match.' In moments
The explosion has forgotten us.
It wonders how it came to be;
Invents a system of belief;
Evolves into a pall of smoke
While we go on demanding
Other universes. 'Quickly, strike –
While we still have the matches.'

Cobain

You had driven west to put geography
Between yourself and my bleak humours. I
Was stunned by news, received in solitude:
Cobain had pulled a trigger on himself,
The pills and whiskey incident, a dress rehearsal rag.

Now, his wife and daughter desolate,
His mother had proclaimed her son
A member of that stupid club.

I'd only known his music, but I'd heard
His double-barrelled blow inside my skull
As morning light rays, April-harsh,
Attempted trepanation on my head,
To disperse the airs that seeped into my lobes
And threatened bad-demeanour meningitis.

I announced it to the first poor soul I found,
A shop hand who stared, innocently blank,
His digits probed by the checkout laser beam.

That night, as black-clad teenage acolytes
Congregated at the cross in Phoenix Park,
I kept internal vigil for a love
That, limping, had been put to sleep like some
Lame horse who faced the hypodermic and
The pasture of the dark: a kind of virtual
Euthanasia. We had buried it still breathing.

Suddenly, the world had flattened
Wide without a *Rough Guide* to the heart,
An atlas of the spinal cord,
A route map of the nervous system.

Banns

You will marry your man on an African beach,
The minister booked, your parents informed,
Your silver dress bought.

Now, the bridal bouquet's
Still a far-flung plantation of seeds –
But I can imagine your long limousine

Taking the sun like a veil on the chrome,
You and your man in the warm leather seat,
As the season of goodwill approaches:

Stone-splitting there, the usual hoarfrost up here
Where tinsel is hung on the neck of the tree
Like a noose killing off the old year.

When you return in the spring of the new,
Your conjugal bliss will insist on its place
In a world that is altered.

Hope of Ray

Thirty six months to the day since we split,
In my sea-facing flat, the shower is blocked
With the hair of a woman not you, but herself –
And I love that long tangle of strands I pulled out.

This morning, she's resting. The comet's asleep
But the sun is awake. I am sprinkling boiled eggs
With black pepper, ground up. I am toasting
McCambridge's stone-wheat brown bread.

Later today we will go window shopping.
Tomorrow we might take a stroll on the beach
Or head for the cinema, there in the dark
Watching other lives spin their tales out.

Easter Comet

In New York you had contracted poison ivy.
Undeterred, you wandered Broadway in a night-dress.

This image of you, fearless of the muggers, jugglers, yuppie
    scumbags,
Comes to me tonight as I stare, standing on my front step,
Up at Hale-Bopp in the northern sky:

A portent of the plague in other ages, but in this,
An imperfection in the firmament,
Across from what is now a bloated moon
That runs fat rays into the clouds
And seems to call: 'My jaundiced skin!'
As though the sky has run off with some luminous
    new stranger.

Those clouds will drift and scatter over your side of the city
Till some hour of the morning when the sky begins to
    lighten. Now
The tide is rolling out. The sea goes on into the dark
Beyond lighthouses.

I Loved You Here

It made him smile, her face when it returned
Without her body or the bottom of her chin.

You can burn and tear and throw them in the trash,
She told him then, but some will not stay dead.

He'd snapped one day a year before;
Removed what she had left behind.

The postcard – Horst P. Horst –
That she had hidden in his pillowcase:
I loved you here, in eyebrow pencil, cursive on the back,
The woman in her corsetry, unbound.

He balled her letters, burnt the lock
Of hair she'd mailed to compensate
For lack of her. The smoke became her ghost.

Her emails, he erased for all their suicidal tenderness
And casual demands
For neat shampoo you could not get abroad.

He threw away the books she'd given:
Walker Percy, Annie Dillard, H.R. Giger, James Agee –
Her taste had been impeccable and probably still was.

He found a note inside the fridge.
I loved you here or hereabouts –
The kitchen at whose table they had dined
On one another. He discarded all discovered relics
But her silken head-scarf that he'd accidentally
Laundered so it held her scent no longer.

Then the photographs. The ones in frames he left
Until he'd burnt the others in their pockets,
Quickly, without looking – dropping them aflame
Into a cooking pot and slapping down the lid;
Switching off the mains in case the fire alarm
Would carry their death-wail upon the air –
And when their wisps had been absorbed,
He let the ashes sail into the street.

He took her portraits from the walls and stuck
A breadknife in their backs and prised the pictures out.
He stuffed the frames into the bin.
He made confetti of the prints.

One year on, her face came back, or part of it.
He smiled as though he'd recently learned how,
The use of his lips almost fully restored,
As after a long-ago crash.

Now, the pictures he'd destroyed were in his head.
He was the frame. For all of those sections of time
That contained a mere segment of her face, he had
Never captured her, had never understood that it
Takes two to make a photograph, that the shooter
Must focus on another, lest he look into himself
And recognise the image he's become.

Sunlit in the burren with a purple car behind her –
I loved you here.

Wearing his green woollen jumper in Paris –
I loved you here.

Holding her nose as they forded at Ha'penny Bridge –
I loved you here.

Windows on the World

High above a passing bird, I sank a Gibson cocktail. I was
Bloodless from a perforated heart and wanted something
To replace the squandered fluid; felt the lure of mental illness – just

The other side of that too solid window, I could catapult – but
Madness seemed like tiger balm, despair like acupuncture, so
I watched the evening terminator trailing blinking lights along

The night-devouring island to the twilight-loving Park. Up here,
My local drinking buddy, getting over someone too, was drawing
Street plans on a napkin. She was down there in those canyons,

He said, breaking hearts and traffic lights, accepting serenades
From stunned New Yorkers and their girlfriends. Then, I think we
Drank a toast to her, and raised a glass in praise of feeling low.

Post-Mortem

I see you on a mortuary slab,
Your blue body bloated.

They've fished you out of the river Don,
Removed your clothes and wrapped you in a sheet.

There is no doubt it's you. There are a thousand
Men out there who could identify your body.

Your hair crowns a high forehead.
Below, a frozen smile –

You are daring the pathologist
To join you in a cold embrace

So that the moment he has gone,
You can feel abandoned.

Then you'll tell me how it was,
How he wouldn't come inside you,

But preferred to spill his seed
Between your breasts,

And how his ribcage was so thick
You could not reach his heart,

And how, when you said 'love,'
He ran, refused to take your calls,

And came back in the morning
With his scalpel and his speculum.

Mercy Fuck

What once was a charm
Is a relic now,
The bone of a saint,
Paraded for the curiosity of strangers
Who can never feel the holiness
But still expect the blessing.

We are dead.
We are dead.

Everything we are
Is a flame
Lost in the furnace
Of time.

I do not care
What we do tonight.
Come here to me. Come here.

Covetous Foetus

I want your life. I want
Your car. I want your
Job.

I want your joy in waking up
Each morning with my mother.

I want your smile.
I want to know
What it felt like
To make me.

I want to get drunk.
I want to take drugs.
I want breast milk laced with cyanide.

I want to jump off
The spire of the *Duomo*
To fall on sunbathers
On rooftop patios below.

I want a sunset on another world.
I want to take her breasts away from you.
I want an abortion.

Rain

Once, after a bout of heavy rain,
I walked the streets of Paris for the kick
Of catching lovers kissing in their doors –
There were none that I could find.

> Maybe, in this town, the act of kissing
> Cloaks you in a shade of grain and glass.

I searched for clues. A woman,
Testing perfumes in *Samaritaine*,
Hovered over atomised chrysanthemums,
Then walked into a cloud, the ghostly
Molecules attracting still, though flowers
And their bees were long deceased.

> Maybe, in this town, the act of dying
> Cloaks you in a shade of love and scent.

Outside, a pregnant woman
With a pit bull like a ball-and-chain
Gave her dog a toilet break
Upon a sapling pushing through the stone
Then tugged on him as though he were
A human child, and dog-piss, lemonade.

> Maybe in this town the act of loving
> Cloaks you in a shade of hope and pain.

An old man wearing better clothes than mine,
Appearing casually spiritual
And godless in the same small frown,
Watched a younger man and woman
Intimate their mutual claim
With hands dug deep inside each other's
Pockets as they promenaded.

    Maybe, in this town, the act of yearning
    Cloaks you in a shade of blues and death.

The cinemas in Montparnasse
Were showing English-language tales
Of love in the original
American. I did not feel
Like following the titles – so
I went in search of raindrops
Still intact upon the paving stones.

    Maybe, in this town, the act of falling
    Cloaks you in a shade of air and speed.

Moon Sea Time

Some irregular night hour. The moon, anaemic, low-slung
In the tide of tissue-cumulus soft-circulating
Upwards toward an atmosphere dissolve. I take my instruments –
A pair of black binoculars and camera – outdoors to the sky: a star
Field trip, over to the barrier that breaks the Irish sea before
It's able to ingest the terraced houses in small increments.

I think of your low white-corpuscle count – the doctor
Told you yesterday – while up there hangs the moon,
Not running red, as in some prophecy of death,
But ashen-faced, its craters clear as to an
Astronaut in orbit of its changeless body; smaller, though,
As fits a man who's never left the Earth.

They say that when our time is gone, when every human
Being has evolved into some other form, and when
The Earth itself has died, and when the moon
Awaits that final flare of nuclear fire – as the solar system
Gasps expiring breath; they say what will remain
Of us are footprints in the lunar dust, without a sea to swallow them.

Spiders

The spiders came from nowhere, spiralling out
Beyond the edge of an under-printed
Chinese take-out flyer in the hall: negative stars
In a transient anti-horoscope.

Later, they were gone. I thought
A neighbour had dispatched them with a pan,
But maybe they had crawled up to the capital,
Enrolled in Spider College, reading: *Engineering 101,
Parachuting for Beginners, Architecture of the Web,
Intimate Geometry, Unpopular Mechanics* –

And got on very well. I think they discovered
A coven of gigantic ants, practicing a magic
Ineffective against venom, spinner, silk. And now,
On summer nights, when I am going down on some
Found Art In A Black Dress, I imagine that the spiders spy –
Scrawling notes on what to do if they should meet a fly.

Sea of Tranquillity

He came home from the party.
In his pocket was the satin star
He'd plucked from decorations.

He woke his daughter, not yet four years old.
He took her, drowsing, out into the road.

He pointed at the sky: the gap
Between Orion's shoulder blades.

'You see that space above the clouds?
I got a great long ladder, laid
The top rung on the moon,
And caught this star that now I give to you.'

Music Downstairs

Songbirds are long gone. The day is old.
I lie awake and naked in your bed.
You pop downstairs to put the kettle on.

Instead, you are diverted by the Steinway
In the living room. You never moved it when
You moved away from here, your parents' home.

And now –
The trickle of a Chopin polka
Rises like a rainstorm in reverse.

Later, over tea, you tell me:
Teachers never heard the music,
Just the notes you missed. It made you

Hesitant about your gift.
You put it down an age ago,
An age at which you could have gone
To Moscow.

Eidolon

Years go by and all your loves devolve into a composite,
Passing on time's travelator, gliding to a terminal,
Never to be seen again and you watch from Security,
Frisked as though this stood for sex, this stood for *intimate*.

Ghosts – and you are ignorant of exorcism rites.
Whenever you're entangled in some temporary angel
Comes the shadow of another love: a flicker of a dimple
Or the first arrested syllable of laughter soft as promises.

You meet her in Departures after half a decade lost
And it's no longer her but her extrapolated. Someone
Calls her over – time to make the plane – and flings
A prophylactic glance at you, you melancholy revenant.

Cicatrice

You did not see mine, on the first night we met.
You were occupied, putting your hand
Through my window, not feeling the pain,
Bleeding your wrist on invisible shards
As you opened the frame just a crack for some air,
Letting autumn leaves in from the fingers of trees.
At some point, we made love, or a bungled attempt.
By the morning, your blood had congealed.

Wounded and practical, no broken bird,
You tried often to show me how two falling leaves
Might collide in the rain, on a current, and sail
As one leaf. In the end, winter rattled us loose.
Now and then, subtle scars raise a sign on my skin
That you left more in me than I ever let on.

Tunisia, Winter 1998

for Yvonne

Tonight, in moonlight, your pellucid skin
Is gleaming as a silent movie star's,
Open lips caressed by playful rays.
Between the jet-black comma of your hair
And the Berber blanket's fringe
That frame your beautiful face like a still –
Your complexion is so clear as to be luminous
As moonlight itself on the crown of a nimbus.

In weeks, all we'll have of each other is desert –
A couple of jars filled with camel-ride sand.
Now, I watch over your dreaming – secure
For the moment, unsleeping but drowsy,
My bare arm exposed at the edge of the bed
That is furthest away from your body:
By the time the mosquito – proboscis drawn in –
Is aware of your breath, she'll have taken her fill.

from
A Shopping Mall on Mars
(2008)

Empire Diner

Muhammad sauntered in and ordered
Peace.

Jehovah rumbled in and ordered
Love.

Jesus Christ strode in and ordered
Hope.

Confucius wandered in and ordered
Brotherhood.

Gandhi shuffled in and ordered
– With a tiny smirk –
Western civilization.

The Buddha floated in and ordered
Everything and Nothing.

Then, a Special Ops brigade,
Crashing through the windows, ordered
Everybody on the floor.

The soldiers opened fire, killing
One wise man, one prince of Time, a godhead and
    three prophets,

A waitress in a uniform, suspected of collaborating
With the old regime –

And a burger-flipping alien
Who had threatened them with a spatula.

Nostalgia

> *'My fellow Americans, I'm pleased to tell you today that I've signed legislation that will outlaw Russia forever. We begin bombing in five minutes.'*
>   – RONALD REAGAN, August 1984

With the last drop of juice in the batteries
Came the voice: a septuagenarian president
Declaring war. Then our radio went dead.

We could not figure, in this pasture where
We'd pitched camp for a summer week,
If there was substance in the air
Of mild amusement in his voice.
Was he around the twist?

We cut sticks for a fire and sat around it,
Two of us warming our cold hands and faces.
Smoke rose. Fire crackled. Sticks spit resin.

Would they land while we were sleeping,
Those protective-suited government officials,
Armoured knights of some new feudal age?

We did not sleep that night and
Come the dawn, we reckoned:
Out here we are safe, but for how long?

That fine, slow, powdered fall from Washington,
That dust migrating south towards our bivouac
Would get us, even if we heard no missile roar,
Or saw no vapour trails:
Horsepower of the Apocalypse.

You suggested that we pack what food we had,
Strike camp and take the car.
'In any case, we're goners,
So we might as well go out amongst our own.'

The landscape seemed unblemished, country
Lanes unspoilt by bodies of dead
Sheep and cattle, dead civilians, horses.

We were bearing up. As building after out-
Building went by, we wondered if a neutron bomb
Had been deployed, no dead outdoors.
It was only in a town that we found out:

The war had not occurred. The former
Actor had been improvising. Testing
Out a microphone, he'd joked about the one thing that
We'd kill him for, should we be, come the moment,
    close enough.

Skydiving Narcissus

Rush of air. The hatch sucked in its cheeks.
A steward pushed him skyward
And the aircraft, lighter by a sigh,
Blew a trail of kisses in its wake.

A baby boom of blushes born in air,
A legend wombed in silk, he pulled his cord.
But, stillborn as his parachute refused,
He had to think, and fast. Relief –
His shoes were fine. They would not look
Improper on the peacocks of Milan.

Then, before the hill-encrusted ground
Presumed to hug his delicate remains,
He prayed that down below he'd find a lake
And knew that he would make a gorgeous corpse.

Turing's Apple

It was only after he had shared his knowledge
That he ate the poisoned fruit.

The garden, having no more use for him,
Destroyed the one who made the weapon sharp,

Dissolved the bond of love that spoke in code,
Denied the secret namer of the world.

Glossolalia

In his teenage years, the kid can speak in tongues.
He feels such peace as he has never known.

And when it's over,
When the preacher has moved on
And when the kid has reached his twenties
And discovered women,
Booze,
And women,
Booze
And women –

His pleasure is tempered by the certainty that
He is damned,
Because the tongues –

Those glottal *aides-mémoires* to one true prayer,
Delivered to a Bronze Age tribe: an oddly ululating code
The devil and his lawyers cannot crack –

The tongues are no longer
Speaking his language.

So –

He searches for their avatar
In every mouth he comes across.

Style Goddess

You had a fondness for the uniforms,
Though not, it must be noted,
For the men themselves. You said that
God might love a sinner's outfit
Though he hate the sinner. So you praised
The Nazis' taste in jackboots, yet
You loathed those whose taste it was.
I wondered if you would admire
The wrapping on a bar of soap
Reduced from Dachau pulchritude.

A Shopping Mall on Mars

'We do not know where this journey will end, yet we know this: human beings are headed into the cosmos.'
– GEORGE W. BUSH, 2004

Out beneath the auspices of Deimos,
Lovers tease each other's lips
In pressurised Buckminster-tents.
They're waiting for the dust to settle.
Then they'll venture back to where
The Habitation billows –
To recover from a long day
At the hydroponics factory.

Once, they'd have imagined this:
Gliding in the sky above *Utopia Planitia,*
Engineers in shuttlecraft
Repairing Aztec-plating
On the starship *Enterprise*
Gripped within the scaffold
Of a skeletal, low-orbit yard.

But now, no one remembers them,
Those pulpish dreams redundant
In a place where Wells's tripod-borne
Unsympathetic eyes are dead;
Where vast and cool intelligences
Open church and shopping mall.

Inversion Ward

At two the moon woke him. He stirred in the bed,
Looked out of the window, the shutters wide open.
The Sea of Tranquillity shone on his head.

The moon seemed to tell him that he had forgotten
His life in a drip, in a room, in the ward.
Like a blue tit that leaves a dead cat at your gate;

A grave robber raised by a time-decayed carcass;
A terrier pissed on by grass blades in mist;
A four-carriage tube train that boards its commuters;

A moon gone insane with the pull of a nutcase;
A lethal injection destroyed by an inmate;
A sun-drenched piazza that visits a tourist;

A knife-wielding cow chowing down on a butcher;
A sign misdirected by a mischievous hitcher;
A mother new-born of the wombs of her daughters –

He had seen yellow skin through his own jaundiced eyes,
That man with blue cotton apparel upon him
Whose nurse, telling lies, made assurances that

He would live to see summer, refusing him smokes
(They were bad for his health) and enduring his chat,
Knew that the Earth would now shine on the sun,

That water would drain down the sink anti-clockwise,
That birds would flap north as his spirit out-flew them,
That soon he would smell only kidney and urine.

His telephone change would run out as he spoke.

Drown

Put your feet down in the iron sea.
Allow the silt to sift between your toes.
Watch out for crabs and sharp sea stones.
Let your legs float free, lie back
Into the arms of Mother Ocean. Take
Your head out of the sky and through
The membrane where it meets the water's
Ever-changing surfaces.

Listen with your inner ear. Your heart
Beat in this underworld sounds
Not from deep inside yourself, but from
The deep itself: a pounding in the water
Like the sonic boom in air, each hit
A signal that you've swum below
The range of human hearing, you've dived darker
Than the eye allows the measurement of light.

Now, let water take you on beyond the limit of the tide –
Farther than the shelf and its old ossifying forms;
Past the point where nature fuses atoms into molecules.

Go into the true deep, to that place
Where latitude and longitude diverge,
Where life is not to be contained. In these
Uncharted depths, where sea has slipped co-ordinates,
Your body is a bottle and your memory's a message
That may find a breaker of its code.

I will go now to the shore
And watch you take on water.
I will wait and watch for your return
As seahorse or anemone –
Or as a vial, drowning and delivered of the word.

Wave Collapse

He finished one last cigarette,
Flicked it and followed it in.

Committed to the deep end,
What shocked him now was not
The unexpected cold but how
His chest, constricted, caved.

Soon out of confidence and breath,
He groped for the rim of the pool –
Within each grasp, a stroke.

The edge bobbed up and down,
A shutter segment teasing out
The terminal impression for
The snapshot of a wave.

Monday, the pool-cleaner found
A pair of identical bodies, both dead.

One of them vanished in front of his eyes.

Descent

It was too late for a pulse to gather.
No blood would carry what remained.
No heart would pump it.

In the lungs there was a stillness
As an inhalation, incomplete,
Hung stranded in the alveoli.

Now they had no name for him.
He had no mark below the neck.

But –

Printed on the inside of his collarbone in braille:

Wash below a certain temperature.
Do not crease and do not iron.

This fallen man belongs to_____

If discovered, please return to_____

To a House of Tin and Timber

Grant McLennan dead at forty-eight –
A heart attack, in bed, in his home town,
That evening's party now become a wake.

Songs are strewn around him
Like invisible petals:
Roses for lyrics, lilies for notes.

The chorus comes later –

A sound that reaches back into the earth
To bloom again in someone else's ears
But never heard the same as when he sang.

I recall a schoolboy coming home

The Philosopher Dances

In memory of Mairead Costigan

'I would not know what the spirit of a philosopher might wish more to be than a good dancer.'
— Friedrich Nietzsche

There is a moment when we stand
Before a mockup of the Shuttle
At the NASA base in Moffett Field.
You speak of the Platonic —
That all we know is only a reflection
Of some higher truth; our finest achievement
Only a clue to some greater endeavour.
Our senses imperfect, we live in the world.

To dance between a man and the essence of Man,
Between a woman and the essence of Woman,
Between a flower and the essence of Flower,
You bring back a note from the garden of Time —
But you love earthly music, equating it with higher math,
The beauty of the universe, the spirit of philosophy.

from
The Darwin Vampires
(2010)

The Darwin Vampires

for Catherine

Being loth to sink in at your neck, they prefer to drink
Between your toes. They revel in the feet; they especially
Enjoy those places in between, where microbial kingdoms,
Overthrown with a pessary, render needle-toothed
Injuries invisible; where any trace of ingress, lost in the fold,

Is conspicuous – as they themselves in daylight are –
By its absence. You will hardly notice that small
Sting; might not miss a drop until the moment
That the very last is drained. And when you're six
Beneath the topsoil, you will never rise to join them.

Rather, you will be a hint; a fluctuating butterfly;
A taste-regret on someone's tongue; a sudden tinted
Droplet in the iris of a fading smile; a blush upon
A woman's rose; a broken vein in someone's eyelid –
Always one degree below what's needed to be warm.

La Femme Éperdue

In this shopworn universe, it seems
That you're the only pristine thing:

You in my blue cotton shirt
Unbuttoned to your navel, who
Perhaps consider me a man

Ephemeral – a sorbet – as you
Mentally re-dress me then take
Seconds in the bathroom.

If there is a god, he never had
The chance to ruin you.
For once, he's not Caligula

Bestowing that raw gift upon
The groom and his intended
In the hour before they wed

So they must stumble to the altar
With his semen slick and motile
On their thighs.

The Mourning Doves

Not long after Ealing,
   I walk the path to school,
      Whistling low to nobody,

Trailing a hand out gently
   To enfold the little fingers
      Of a boy who is not there.

I leave him at the open gate.
   I bend to kiss the boy a breath
      Of love and fortune on his brow.

That same afternoon I return
   To bring the boy, my firstborn, home
      For the first time.

There, although the mourning doves
   Coo solemn recognition,
      His mother does not know
         She is a mother.

Husk

If tonight by some mistake I end up eating you
As though you were a human madeleine,
The rush of memory alone

Might charge my system like a toxin,
Thrust me back inside the life
I knew when I was innocent.

The one with whom I once had formed
A matching pair, I cannot wholly conjure now.
The lightbulbs in our common house have blown.

Yet you are here, a living counterfeit;
A ghost incarnate; some unwitting cameo.
You would not know me from a psychopath.

Now should I mix you one part sorrow,
Two parts trouble, garnished with
A twist of disappointment,

Would you let me cut into your life
And ask why you are out alone,
And could you use a compliment?

And how is it you have her hair,
That raven helmet of a bob?
And what have you done with her face?

You almost have her smile. It sits
Improper on your lips, a slit
Impertinent, dividing Rimmel pink.

I watch you taking over. You, emergent, sap
The pale declining essence of her memory,
Becoming into fullness. When you're through,

You are a hollow reproduction with no soul;
An almost faithful replica I cannot lay a finger on,
For if I break you, perfect stranger, I will own you.

Love Watches for Death

I

Love watches for Death. She watches the road.
She waits for her Death to come home.

When he does, he is mute. He must keep his own counsel
Regarding his time in the desert

In order that he does not burden her conscience
With knowledge of deeds he has done in her name.

II

Love watches for Death. She waits for her stud
To come home to their bed, for she misses his touch;

She's deprived of the heat of a body that's rightfully hers;
And wasn't she promised the comfort and strength of a man?

III

Love watches for Death. When her Death returns home
He says nothing to Love of the children he's maimed;

Of the men he has burned so a town could be saved.
If he tells her the truth of it though he can barely

Believe it himself, she'll disown him as some kind of
Changeling. When Death

Gives not even a word;
When he fails to expose the old stain on his heart

So that she can consider her own unbesmirched,
Love denounces his silence

And Death
– Without a defence against Love's disappointment –

Takes to the desert again,
In search of a quantum of peace.

Baby

We buried one small shoe in the ground.
We waited for the rain and watched it pour.

The tongue came first, a toughened shoot
That grew into a leather trunk and sprouted

Laces for branches. Then the branches split
And limbs snaked out – spindles of flesh.

Part-formed mouth and fragment of eye;
Here the beginning of a rib, there the start

Of a lung – elsewhere half a heart, half-beating;
Somewhere in among all this, the mazes of a brain.

A misshapen body knitted from the cords of living
Tissue, barked in leather, nameless, dragged itself

Out of the crust of the soil that was rejecting it
Even as it tried to smile and let us know it loved us.

Something close to a child attempted to lurch
Towards us but was dead before it took a step.

We watched it fall, this thing that we had made,
But we could not look for long.

We left its remains to fester in the field,
Slowly to descend into the cold, affronted earth.

Skywalker Country

It was a long time ago. The boy was out
On the bog with a ruddy neighbour, a man
Strawberry-faced from years of hidden anger
And pious disgust at every foreign thing.
Although he'd brought a radio he tolerated
For the Gaelic, he remained dismissive

Of transmissions from abroad. Now while
The neighbour passed remarks and fed on bacon
Sandwiches and hearkened to the news hour
And the Angelus, the boy piled up a rick
For grown-ups to bring later in their trucks.
The day wore on. Another programme started:

Star Wars from the NPR. This was no bog,
But Tattooine. And to a man
For whom Drumshanbo was too far,
Mos Eisley was unthinkable. 'American muck,'
He said, and turned it off. He urged the boy
To pray, and save himself as well as turf.

Saint Dracula

Louis Jourdan's Count played
On the BBC that night.

The Christmas spirit was undead.
The boy had just found out
Santa was a lie his parents told.

Insomniac with vampire dread,
He worried all that now remained
Were Dracula and God.

Both had risen from the grave.
Each demanded: 'Drink my blood
And live forever as my slave.'

It wasn't looking good
For 1978.

Crush

The hottest-ever summer. I am seven.
Out on the step, my aunt is reading a paper.
I ask her why that 'i' is upside-down.
It is an exclamation mark, she says.

My mother's friend arrives with her daughter.
For a photograph, the adults make us kiss.

I am captured in short pants;
My hair is pageboy chic; my tank top
Over wide-necked purple shirt,
Sports orange stripes on brown.
I'm like a walking Bridget Riley.

I remember the girl's hair.
It is flowing black.
Her face is all squinting embarrassment.

That kiss and one upended 'i'
Begin the shortening of days.

Into the moment when a life discovers time
– The borders between birth and dying fixed –
Experience accelerates, succumbs:

Gradually crushed
As if a sound explosion turned,
Compacted in a singularity of memory,
Subsumed as single notes,
Each of which had once discretely rung
Grander than an opera.

Junky

I had known that when I got to thirty-two,
  In the year of the millennium,
    We would all have flying cars.

      In a corner of the bedroom
      He pulled back the linoleum,
      Discovered the controls of a rocket
      And became again that five-year-old
      Working with crayons.

We'd float in sky hotels the shape of wheels;
  Or live in giant city-domes
    Protected by a shield from meteorites.

      Constructing a spacecraft
      To carry him up there,
      Far above the clouds,
      The boy had drawn buttons,
      A viewscreen, a joystick,
      Shaded in orange and purple and black.
      Everything worked.

We'd all pop pills instead of dinner –
  But there would always be ice cream;
    They'd be selling Klondikes on the moon.

      Eventually forgotten,
      That homemade control room:
      As years counted down, it became
      A fossil record of the future,
      Its cargo of notions adrift,
      The rocketship lost under lino,
      Wrecked on the coral of spacetime.

Freakchild

Running in the street
& the house is on fire &

Knowing that I was the one
Who left the oven on &

Grandad is asleep
Or will be till the smoke

Grabs him by the throat &
Flings him around the room

Before he melts from
Beating back the flames,

I wonder what's the deal
With all that noise &

That commotion.
Is the fire truck arrived already? Wow.

The Golden Age of Aviation

On his early transatlantic flights, he could smoke in the cabin
And drink as much as he liked and it was free although he wasn't even
In First. In those days, they didn't think about getting it in the alveoli
Because who knew then that cigarettes were evil; not to mention that
Everyone was in for it eventually, so why not enjoy the party?
It wasn't as though you could pop outside for a sneaky Camel Light.

Besides, there were other deadly activities that could be performed on
Aircraft, such as sex in the toilets; such as flying itself; such as hitting
A mountain or another plane. A UFO, should one pass by, was unlikely
To fry the controls with an electromagnetic pulse, but Armageddon
Might break out at any moment, because this was the nineteen-eighties
And there were oceans of oil on tap to fire up the engines of Pershings.

The cell-phone had not become popular yet and no
  one had digital devices
Which could interfere with the signals the nervous-
  system of the Boeing
Sent along itself to keep the great preposterous thing
  within its heavier-than-air
Suspension of disbelief – but there was always the
  chance that a Baader-
Meinhof splinter group might storm the cockpit and,
  with menaces,
Demand the pilot drop this bird in somewhere
  communist and foreign.

The smoke from cigarettes of course detracted from the
  taste of airline food
Which, contrary to ill-informed opinion, was in fact
  delicious and quite good.

4°

Clouds of mirrors in orbit
Turn the face of the sun
Away from the Amazon desert

    The Lost City of Barcelona
    The Lost City of Mumbai
    The Lost City of New York

The submerged hulls of the Sydney Opera House
Like an experimental cruiser seen from below
An inverted waterline

    The Lost City of Berlin
    The Lost City of Cape Town
    The Lost City of San Francisco

A billion human bodies
Abandoned in the dunes
Of Italy and France

    The Lost City of Galway
    The Lost City of Beijing
    The Lost City of Memphis

The Greenland Arcologies reach for the sky
The Antarctic Riviera opens for the season
The Roman Sahara reconquers an empire of dust

    The Lost City of Zurich
    The Lost City of Islamabad
    The Lost City of Atlanta

4' 33"

After the
    Planes
The only music to be heard
    In those elevator carriages
Is Cage's.

Reflecting Angel

When they started talking back, their voices
Chiming in without permission, first came
A charismatic mother, branding him a lamb,
Abandoned on an endless plain of loneliness.

The devil had clearly deprived him of light –
So she offered him a drop of something pure,
Lifted Stolichnaya from the kitchen floor.
She'd stashed it by her perforated feet.

Right in front of him she poured out two
Full measures for herself and hid the bottle;
Drained her hand of vodka neat and subtle;
Whispered, 'All I'm worried for is you.'

He blinked and in the room was no one else.
His blinded eyes stared back into his face.

You Murder the Sun

You murder Tchaikovsky. You used to love
His *Violin Concerto in D*, the Kennedy version.
Something in Pyotr's martyrdom appealed to you.
His final symphony you loved as well, felt his use
Of *Pathétique* was anything but modesty.

You murder *Rhapsody in Blue*.
You murder *Manhattan*.
You murder Woody Allen.

You murder the epsilon at work
Who sniped that he had never met anyone
Quite as incontinent as you.
He had meant to say 'incompetent'.

You murder every grain of sand.
You murder every particle of water in the sea.
You murder every tree in the park.

You murder all the clouds
That ever passed above your head,
Telling you of elephants and Russia.

You murder dark matter.
You murder the moon.
You murder Australia.

You murder the night you made love
In a lightstorm with Y.,
Daring the bolts to incinerate you both.
When you lived, you promised that next time
You would do without the lightning.
That would show it.

You murder the sunshine that made G.'s wedding day
Angelic as *A Convent Garden, Brittany*.

You murder William Leech.
You murder the sun.
You murder all weddings.

You murder all funerals.
You murder the ones who went before
And showed you how it's done.

You murder that old tourist who,
Over mojitos in Bar St Germain,
Let slip that one fall afternoon as a girl,
She trained the neighbours' Labrador
To lap her up
Into a perfect, frothing O.

You murder the Heisenberg Uncertainty Principle.
You murder the teleportation of quantum states.
You murder the Sombrero galaxy.

You murder the Neapolitan assault of pleasure
When you put anchovies, capers and green olives
In the same mouth at the same time.

You murder *A Death in the Family*.
You murder *Nineteen Eighty-Four*.
You murder *I Am Legend*.

You murder your surprise at the Olympia when S.,
Returning from the ladies' room post-interval,
Found herself caught up in the stageward procession
Of the Polyphonic Spree.

You murder the Golden Gate Bridge in 1995.
You murder the Piazza del Campo in 1996.
You murder Port El Kantaoui in 1998.

You murder the receptors in your memory flesh,
Each existing now
Only for the loss it represents –
Time and place
Translated into chemicals.

                                          At random:

Someone you had loved,
Split off into another life,

A universe
You know nothing about.

All you have is the recording.
You murder even that.

Time for the two of you
Stopped.

It stopped everything happening
At once.

Time.
You murder time.

It is all you can do
To kill it before it kills you.

Hidradenitis Suppurativa

Subcutaneous for months,
A jet of pus and blood
Arced across the room
From a swelling in my thigh.
The stain persisted on the wall.
I had shot the house
With an anti-decoration gun
The size of a year.

Counting backwards on a table,
Breathing in a blackout.
Seconds later, coming to,
Having mislaid a whole morning.

On television in the ward, an astronaut,
Returned three decades from the moon,
Recalled the effect on his marriage
Of discovering unforeseen meaning
In the word 'anticlimax'.

A nurse brought a limp tuna sandwich.
The bread was a poultice
Ready to draw the dead fish back to life.

I picked at my stitched, bandaged
Groin. Under the bondage of gauze,
Surgical thread, like trainee barbed wire,
Puckered the lips of the wound,
Making it kiss itself better.

Anaphylaxis

Solitude, like water, was something he decided
He needed more of but when he went in search of it,
He discovered that, like potable water, there seemed to be
Less of it about, as though there'd been a convention
Of thirsty hermits in the vicinity of his home and
They'd bottled all the silence. So he drove to the beach
At midnight, found the remains of jellyfish, alien ghosts,
An apocalypse of invertebrates, whose stings lay in wait
For him to make contact. He saw no people in this place
Where one time, naked hundreds had posed for photographs,
Some drunk and freezing pink in the Irish summer dawn.
He considered walking in the water in the dark, diluting
Himself like a poison on its current, out past the buoys.
By the time he got to Portishead, full of brine and tangled
Up in random junk from some rich waster's luxury island,
He would himself be jetsam. But the sea was crowded too.
And looking out into the galaxy, he found no reassurance:
Every place was full. Even all the dark between the stars
Was matter now, not vacuum; trillions unlike anything
He could begin to contemplate lived there. It was no good.
He took off both his shoes – and stepped into a jellyfish.

Manila Hemp

If I had been you —

I'd have checked the trapdoor and release
For proper operation. I'd have
Soaked and stretched the rope
To rule out spring or coiling. I'd have
Oiled the hangman's knot
For smoother sliding.

Tied around a grommet and a bracket,
The rope prepared to take the sudden
Weight and force of someone's fall;
Measurements, examinations, aiding
In avoiding strangulation or
Beheading —

That is how I would have done it.

But you were never me
And when you did it, you had no
Technique; you'd no finesse.

Your drop continued, feet-first, into
Other people's lives and through them,
Leaving exit wounds.

The Forest

Were you to drop into a lake
And let the water fill you
Like some premature formaldehyde;
Or take a naked razor in the bath;

Or hang a sudden turn
Into a tram car as it pulled away;
Or crush a ton of sleeping pills,
Dissolve in gin and sip the night in minutes –

You could never quite explain it to your daughter
When she was old enough to understand
The truth of what you'd done.
So let whatever happens, happen.

Soon enough for anyone, it does.
Let nature and caprice become the sniper
No one sees but in whose sights
We all await our inexplicable release.

One day you observe yourself alone
Walking that cold forest in your head.
You never hear the shot. The weapon is not found.
Everything you ever were is buried under snow.

Sooner than the seasons change
There is no trace of you at all.
You are what's forgotten by the ones
Who do not know they have forgotten.

Gloria Mundi

In that recurring future memory,
I push out from the capsule's
Open hatch – my Mercury
Recalling Alan Shepard's.
Snug within a pressure suit,
I'm paid out on the tether line
That tautens until, breaking
Tensile limits, it whips free,
Unleashing an infinity
In which I feel no terror.
Rather, lost in wonder at the sky,
I find a liberation in accepting
That I'll die out here.
There's nowhere I would rather die.
Moreover, beatifically
Mislaid between the moon
And Cape Canaveral,
I revel in being utterly alone,
Elated in my weightlessness –
The last breath in my lungs expelled
To hush a fragile wisp
From that frail atmosphere
Of bygone Earth above where
Nature ever dared to blow.
The flower of an astral ghost,
My final exhalation, leaves
A shrinking mist upon the glass.
Embalmed by space and gliding
Out of orbit, now descending
To cremation-by-re-entry –
I desire within my reverie
To settle on the solar wind,
And float serenely far beyond Centauri.

A Promiscuity of Spines

Volcano Day

Your heartbeat in my ear;
My tear upon your breast –

And in the earth, a thunder
Where there never had been

Thunder. In the street
Where never had we heard

Any more percussion
Than a drum in some god's

Dying day parade –
Arrhythmia, a starting thing

So let it come –
My tear upon your breast;

And let it come –
Your heartbeat in my ear.

Already we are studies
For our own discovered statues.

A Promiscuity of Spines

for Sara

You have a synecdoche dream.
'One day, my dear, it would be sweet;
It would be very fine indeed, one day,

'If all your books and mine
Were stacked against the future,
Packed on the same set of shelves

'Under the same star-proof ceiling,
Somewhere with a mountain
And maybe a lake.'

My Barnes against your Hoban;
Your Mitford on my Matheson –
I get the picture. Good. It's good

And fitting that this should be so. But
There's one thing.
There's just one thing.

I promise that I will not be put out
If among your books I find
A dedication from the past, from

Someone wholly unlike me
But close to what you'd had in mind
Once, before you changed it

Or he changed;
Long before I came to be
Even half a bookmark in your week,

Let alone a finger lightly touching
Yours between the second glass of wine
And everything.

But you may take exception if you like,
To the Miller and its 'velvet kitten kiss' –
For who would welcome that among her Penguins?

That one's gone, the one who wrote those words;
Was gone before her nib was even wet. Off to be
Outstanding in the snow. And yours are gone.

I do not mind their traces and their names.
I do not mind their strokes, their wit, their style,
Flat against the grain.

Visitor

I did not know which one you were.
In my head you kept drowning.

I could not fathom your face –
Not entirely here and not all there.

Some other night you came to me,
In my childhood home, a place

You'd never been. As we embraced,
Wounds bloomed on your forehead,

Your breast; and blue you went, and black –
A walking bruise. I turned to get the phone

And it was you I tried to call; to bring
Me out of there – but caught between

The two of you,
I catapulted from paralysis and woke,

Expecting you to shimmer in the room
Of this hotel on Boston Common. It took cold

Seconds to confirm my solitude;
Took hours to sleep again.

Tonight, you drown and drown again.
Again you drown. I wake alone and wet.

Sleight

Caught in the wonder of it, not caring
To know how such a thing was possible,
We were willing to suspend the laws
Of physics for the sake of the illusion:

The conjuror made *crème de menthe*
Tumble from a teapot. Moments earlier
The spout had given bourbon. In a minute
It would bring forth wine then handkerchiefs.

After the magic was over I killed the evening
By downing Manhattans with my antihistamines
And later still, by falling dead to the night
When you wanted so badly to take me alive.

Come the morning all your young desire
Had turned away. You could not bear the touch
For which you'd only finished yearning. There
Were four more days to go until my flight.

Timing

I

Walking out
In front of yourself
Walking
In front of a car

II

Dodging
The bullet-
Shaped boat
That you missed

III

A gun introduced
In the third act
Is fired
In the first

Glue

The one who, after
Falling off Bucephalus,

Found poor Rocinante
Occupied already —

That one put the saddle
On his own back.

The Lion and the Boy

Ten times and more your height the lion stands
And greater than all terror, fills your eyes.
The man with whom you came has idle hands.

That man in black has burned in foreign lands
To drill the seed of Christ where old god lies.
Ten times and more your height the lion stands.

It stalks a zeal of zebra through grasslands
Parched under sun; savannah for disguise.
The man with whom you came has idle hands.

He's put them to the work his god demands:
To cut the old one's army down to size.
Ten times and more your height the lion stands.

The fire of its mane, those flaming strands
Frame yawning silhouette against sunrise.
The man with whom you came has idle hands.

You tremble in the dark. One zebra lands
With blood spray, flesh torn out. A vulture flies.
Ten times and more your height the lion stands.
The man with whom you came has idle hands.

Winter

Autumn grows the telescopes.

The trees between the buildings
Start to shed their leaves –

Last season's colours,
Summer's unbearable clothes.

Springtime confounds the voyeurs.

Shokushu Goukan

> *'Give me the child until he is seven and I will show you the man.'*
> — IGNATIUS OF LOYOLA (apocryphal)

Suckers on my body as I sleep.
You penetrate my dreams.

You lay your babies in my head
While I,

Behind my vortices of eyes,
Imbibe the ichor from your

Hectocotylus
Sliding in my body

As your three green hearts beat,
Pump my blood.

I swim in you.

Selas

Days when every night is a full moon
And you a true lycanthrope. No doubt
There'll be a dawn; it will not save you.

Dawn will draw you out. It's not the bone-
Distort mutation that reshapes you
In a hail of lunar stabs; it is your shadow

In daylight you hope no one will see. That blot
Of darkness follows you around like a tell –
The wolf unrevealed but his tail on display.

Black Smoke

There is no Australia in the Bible. This point
Gave them resolution when they came.

In the sky that Easter Sunday morning,
A new sun flashed, snuffing out

The Guard in a second, along with everyone
It had been charged with protecting.

What remained was not a city of the dead.
There were no corpses in the streets. Where

They still existed as anything, the people
Were shadows traced on marble walls.

The ceiling of the chapel was unwounded;
The Pythian Apollo, undefiled. Statuary

Inherited this territory,
Contaminated now for centuries.

The Boudoir Grand

Beneath you to observe
That its teeth are kicked in
And its felt is worn out
And its pedals are bent.

Unseemly to admit
Its rusted strings
And weathered pegs
And balding lacquer.

You change your face.
You give up the use of your hands.
Any time you think about it now,
It was never you

Who played the thing at all
But someone else,
Someone for whom you can have
Proper understanding.

The Jerusalem Syndrome

If you can raise a dead man from the grave;
Relieve a leper of his old contagion;

If you can pirouette like Kelly on the waves;
Transmute spring water into Sauvignon;

And conjure from a loaf and half a cod
A picnic for your captive audience –

Possessing such an enviable rod
With which you don't intend to reproduce,

Appears a tad superfluous. That's why
I let them circumcise me as a boy.

Giddy Andromeda

You thought yourself composed of stars –
A hundred billion single points of light
Comprised your body.

No one, on meeting you,
Could tell just how fast you were going.

No one, on watching you move,
Could pinpoint exactly where you were

Or know how you suspected
That your suns were going out,
Not singly but in clusters.

Even you could only
Guess how many regions of yourself

Were dark already,
Or how long you had left.

Nothing to be done but dance
As slowly as you could
Towards the exit.

Brittle Hour

Could you fall away in the dark
Without awareness of your going
You would do it in a heartbeat and a half.

    love
      song
        book
          worm
            wood

The woman of eggshell cracks
Takes you down from the mantel
To clear a path for the Child of Prague;
Its obscene decapitations.

Cut

You marry the knife
That fits the incision

You never let close —
The slit in your side.

When it comes,
Blame the hand.
When it comes —

The slit in your side
You never let close,

That fits the incision —
You marry the knife.

The Orphan

An old man falls down in a field. That's all I have.
I do not know his given name. His family
Name was yours before you wed.

Some old man falls half-nameless
And all I have is your word that he lived
Before he left you to the oversight of others.

Was there rain that day or did the sun parade
A disc behind his head as he collapsed,
Sainting the fallen with a personal eclipse?

Was there a single lightning bolt
That felled him with a crackling inside,
Arteries caving in after years of abuse?

Was it like that? A final crushing day
After weeks of them poured into seconds
Split in the field where falls an old man

Who doesn't get up. You never spoke
Of him except that once. I was then six
Perhaps or four. He had been gone a while

Before I came to you. An old man falls
Down in a field and that is all. In truth
I do not know what age he was.

Elvis still had five
Years left the night you told me.
Kennedy's body was warm in your mind.

But that old man who falls.
For you he's falling now.
His fall became your sundial.

Did he stagger, did he tumble to the furrow
With a hot knife in his arm and chest?
Did he clutch his heart, cry out?

Who, for instance, might the man
Have called for at the end?
His priest? A doctor? You?

And did he drop alone among
The crows, his own cries drowned against the caws; that
Clean air of the rural 1960s, that clean air.

Did he recognise the final breath at last;
And did his stroke shoot through your chambers too
Like reiki gone awry?

He must have lived one moment at the end.
He must have known — but this is all you gave.
An old man falls down in a field. An old man fell.

Apollo

Your newborn on a ventilator.
Three days in. The doctor
Says go home but you will not.

You smoke a roll-up in the corridor
Then wander into the ward
To watch the moon. They have landed,

Those snowmen. Fading out, they remind
You of the ultrasound. It looked
Like the window of an orbiter.

Your little astronaut —
Cradled in a fragile module, suspended
Between one world and another.

The National Style 'O' Resonator

You pass it to him hopefully. 'Play me something
Meaningful. Thrill me on your metal strings
With a blues from my homeland, or the spiritual
You learned how to pluck, just to undress me.'
Fingers adept on a fretboard, you intuit,
May serve you well in other ways. But this –
This is before you are married. This is the time
You desire him the more for his skill with a neck.

There will come a day, after a long intermission,
When he takes the machine out from under the bed,
Shines it like new, carries it down to the kitchen,
Hoping to catch your smile reflected in the body
As his fingers flutter on your lips, trying to strum
The music back into your voice.

The Celluloid Angel

All December long, you built the thing up
Out of *papier-mâché,* and film you had got
From your job at the print works in town.

You ribbed its wings with coat-hanger wire,
Taped over and painted. It was a purple
And silver construction that would never fly

So you made its body frame of wire too,
Plugged into a thick wedge of wood, its feet
Flat like the broken feet of a messenger.

Its head, with hollows for eyes, pointed
At whoever looked into them, seemed
To ask: 'What class of devil are you?'

Those winter nights, as you layered paper
Skin on your growing creation, the telephone
Would ring, a fat black Bakelite box. It would

Bleat and there'd be a voice, breathing, just
Breathing, and it made me afraid that the angel
Was calling the house as you brought it alive.

One night you were ready with a keyboard
You'd set up on your bench by the phone.
When the breathing came, you put the handset

To the speaker, fingered some tusky chord
That must have penetrated, burst the angel's
Drum, for it didn't call once after that.

By the time the creature was complete,
Your paper and wire and celluloid angel,
You left with the others in your band.

I handled the landlord alone and found
The angel abandoned in the empty house.
I took it with me; felt like I'd raided a tomb.

Through two decades it has stood on high
Shelves or low stools, recording every disaster,
Its wings swept back, hoping for a draught

Of secret fire to lift it heavenwards,
But eyeless like the rest of us
And heading for zero, the old wall that waits.

Dragonfly

Nothing will make sense of it. One day all your
Love songs come to seem like overreactions
To misconstructions. *Tsar Bomba* ignited
By a safety match on splints. And even those
Were never redwood; they were barely even timber.

There is no more fire, for nothing demands it.
Your lips and tongue as good as sewn with gut,
Never again will you sing another's miracle.

Your eyes might never blink again for you will risk
Nothing but this: the almost imperceptible,
Continual accretion of photons that layer
Palimpsests of light, without meaning or weight,
Green on top of blue on top of red, darkening

Until your lenses polarise, admitting nothing,
Not even the sky. Your ears burn down the doors
Where once had come in saxophone and rain.

Days

for Mairead Costigan

For the salt, beneath a Madagascan moon, a moth
Supping the tears of a sleeping bird, drawing
Nightmare into his thorax; imagining an egg

Of *Newtonia* ripping the walls of his own velvet body,
Dropping as wings fall away, like an experiment
Of Cayley's gone awry. Does every flying thing

Have tears and dreams? In this first moment
That we meet, we cannot know. Your campus
Holiday-quiet, the Palo Alto bar is hushed. You speak

Of Nietzsche and the Kinks and your guitar.
With Beefheart at the mixing desk it would be
Quite the mad ensemble, wouldn't it?

Nearly shot at Ames for taking photographs;
We later stand in wonder at *The Gates of Hell*.
You overhear a traveller on the train to San Francisco

Ask a beardy stranger if his axe can truly sing. Now
The millennium — the real one — has not broken yet.
Before it can, I'll half-forget what tears are for

And you will have remembered many dreams.
Soon enough I must fly south to Christmas drinks and fish
And chips on Manly Beach. On a clifftop verandah

In Woolloomooloo, I'll probe a vertical curtain of rain.
At the observatory, I'll murmur to Venus, bright as a spirit
Lamp. Overlooking water with your sister and her friends

I'll welcome Arthur Clarke's transcendent year
As rockets fly — and from the harp of the bridge,
A thousand fireworks spit in heaven's eye.

The Idlewild Rose

Jump in the air. Attached
To your bare feet a ghost
Is leaping down and up:

The shadow you don't see. For
Every person living now, said
Clarke, stand thirty ghosts,

Trapped on the flipside
Of that particular life. Take yours
And how they would delight

In having your place in the world
No matter that it got so hard.
But this is no land for the dead,

Troubled as it must remain
By their shades, the living.
Take you. Your friends are dust.

You walk alone but for their
Incognito phantoms listening
In the street tonight. You play

The spoons, you play the spoons –
Clacking them up to my room,
Murdering my sleep in its sleep. I pull

The window open; stick my head
Into your racket like a bum note.
I imagine how you got a part

In this orchestra of one. Some
Beautiful soldier at an airport,
Half a life ago in New York,

Stormed out of your arrangement,
Granted you a last half-hour as his rose
Before pulling the cord —

And that was it. You were done.
Up he flew into another's draft.
You were replaced in your life

By yourself only worse.
Now you're a regular poltergeist
With an irregular ticker

And a chest complaint. Now
There are days when all you want is —
You don't know what you want.

It took you ten years to believe that you
Were not the one who broke his
He(was never broken)art.

Now you are the shade of a shade.
When you met him again that one time
On Sutter his eyes went through

Your face without leaving a tear
And you knew. You were the core
Discarded when the blade was struck.

Ouse

Afloat on the gloss of the river, a pad
Of auburn hair cowls into a head
Rippling up and a coat peels away to expose
A summer dress, pocked by wounded roses.

No hilt in your hand, you emerge –
Drying out in the hazard sun
That rises like a symptom of the day,
Distended in the west above the Downs.

You wade in reverse to the bank. Barefoot
You stand there and pluck nine rocks
Out of your overcoat pockets.

Then you set them all down in a line
On the quickening skin of the land
Like the late, discarded ova of a gargoyle.

Tiberian

No matter that the Emperors are dust,
Rome will have its minnows. All the boy-
Fish nipping at the wretched flesh of dull
Tiberius, could not outshine the body
Of one virgin saint for innocence and purity.

Take this child-bride of the Nazarene. They say
Here is a girl who chose to die before defilement.
Martyred at eleven, she had not attained the age
Even of Lateran consent. Maria we may venerate;
From her beg intercession. Not Tiberius's minnows.

Submerged among the eye-teeth of the boy-fish,
Displacing no more thought than you'd expect,
Tiberius lives on. No matter that the minnows
Come and go, Rome will have its Emperor
And after him, the mad one with the horse.

The *Voyager* Mote

There are no traces, at the edge of deep,
Of chocolate or lilacs, of deathcaps
Or bicycles, of god or schizophrenia,
Of socialist theatre or the kakapo. Nor

Is there evidence at all for the time
Your grandmother settled you, a bairn
On her bony old knee, and told you how
Her father lined his family up, out by the gable,
And cracked a horsewhip, lashed them open –
Daughters, wife and sons – because the Tans
Had smoked his brothers from their cave
And shot them in their heads, and they but lads.

There is no indication whatsoever here
That Brundle discovered insect politics;
That Hedy Lamarr invented Wi-Fi;
That someone *inconnu* first typed *Fin*.

There are no inklings from six billion k
Of the day you were sent with a girl,
To deliver a bucket of milk to a man
In a cottage a mile away, and you barely five.
It took the pair of you to carry the pail.
On the way you saw beyond your world:
The garments of travelling people,
Draped on a dry-stone wall to bake.

Here there is no argument for Mormons,
Or Marilyn Monroe, or Mitochondrial Eve,
Or Mao, or Mary or Moses or midichlorians.
No sign of Martin Luther King or Eminem.

Neither is there any hint out here
Of the student actor who, after you sat down
From speaking in public that very first time,
Reached from behind you with two
Lucky Strikes, both alight; and landed them
Between your lips. It was the beginning
Of your beautiful friendship
With toasted tobacco, and loss.

No evidence of all we are or anything we've done –
Not until you know what it was for,
This flower that sent the misprint planet home,
The period in every question mark.

Background Radiation

Imprinted on the dust I find the vocal remains
Of two who have lived here before me. On top
Of the wardrobe in my new Victorian bedroom:

Melody, don't.

The rockets of their heartbeats
Have collided at the wallpaper barrier,
Forced back into each other and through –

Mating dustballs now,
Locked together
In perpetual equilibrium.

Inches away, sprung from between
The fragments of a broken Dalkon Shield,
More mangled signals:

Melody – I will – don't –
I'll kill you, I swear – wasn't swollen enough –
Mel, just don't – as if your poor head –

Far to the left,
Big as a crumpled stocking,
A meshed ladder of dust emits atmospherics.

Mingled are crickets; a tomcat in heat;
A thrown-wine-glass smash; plaster-crack;
A sewing-machine, gunning a nightshirt;

Water for a copper bath, gurgling in the pipes;
An early television set, shimmering in and out;
Rainstorms and soft morning drizzle;

The wail of a child, perhaps theirs.
That cry is unfinished, hanging wet on the end
Of his mother's last, half-remembered thump.

Now I lift a print of carrier dust.
Vibrations pierce my fingertip
As if to take a sample.

I scatter a cacophony of bloodsong:
Silence interrupted by the slamming of a door –
Its echo shrink-wrapping the contours of a face;

One breath – a slow, corrupted breath –
Failing on a wavelength of raggedness
In the lungs of someone beautiful.

Crystals of falling notes degrade in the lacunae
Between matter and everything else.
By the time the aurora of particles

Dusts down on the floor,
There is nothing at all of those sounds
But an atom-thin carpet of static

Settling on the parquetry, needling
The grain in the wood, attempting
To play itself back from the start.

Acheron

The neverending river
Dreaming in your head

Deposits every moment
On the bed like recovered

Wreckage for you to survey
At your repentant leisure

So that you may see them
All at once. Time contorted

Throws in each memory
You lost and fear. One

Might turn out helpful,
A scenario to demonstrate

What needs to be done
To get you out of here.

There is no getting out.
Pain is what comes now.

You burst with it –
Your life does not parade;

It explodes
In that sun-fathered cranium

Like a hand-grenade
Microwaved by eternity

And you become the shrapnel
That falls into the current —

Settled in the depths until
Filtered in the sediment.

Time strains your entirety
Out of the flow.

The Amnesia-to-Melancholy Ratio

There was a meteorite. Years ago.
Nobody observed it at the time
Though it was mighty as Chicxulub
Strapped to the back of Tunguska.
To most, it just looked like the sky.

It might as well have been Allan Hills –
Tucked away in a lab, studied and stored
Until somebody made the connection
With Martian fossils and for a moment
The scumbayas were petrified.

You didn't feel it then but it knocked
You for six; holed you in a hundred places –
Apertures that undermined your structure
So that Kryptonite was nothing to you now.
You curved as required, mirroring those

Who came into your orbit; taking on
Their shapes; reflecting what they might
Expect. You swerved and pretzelled
For to stand up at all was to risk
Collapse. That meteorite was good.

If one of them had wiped out the dinosaurs,
What had another done to tiny, flightless you,
Not even a terrible lizard? The meteorite
Survived: lately, an unexpected land mass
Has been sighted off the islets of engrams.

Doppelgänger Clues

You wake me with a squeezing
Of strawberry cut – one drop
On my left lid, one drop on my right –
And the tenderest kiss to my nose.

I open my strawberried eyes,
Expecting to find him in the room,
Lotus on the duvet, uncrossing;
Dissolving before I can make out his edges –

But he has not come. I have to
Do this on my own. I know he
Turns up when I am not looking
Out for him. There's evidence.

My beard hair on his razor
In your bathroom cabinet.

His love bruise on your neck
That day in Grace Cathedral Park.

In his mouth, my brutal tongue,
Smarting after you have kissed and bitten it.

THANKS

My gratitude to those who published the books: Jessie Lendennie and Siobhán Hutson at Salmon Poetry for *The New Pornography*, *Breaking Hearts and Traffic Lights* and *The Darwin Vampires*; Dermot Bolger and Aidan Murphy at Raven Arts Press for *Jazztown*; Geoffrey Gatza at BlazeVOX [Books] for *A Shopping Mall on Mars*; and Dennis Greig at Lapwing for *Touchpaper Star* and *Cicatrice*, two chapbooks later incorporated into the main collections.

For encouragement in the early days, thanks to: Macdara Woods and his fellow editors at *Cyphers*; Pat Boran, Theo Dorgan and Rory Brennan at Poetry Ireland in the late 1980s; Eavan Boland at the 1989 National Poetry Workshop; Ciaran Carty at the *Sunday Tribune*; and Heather Brett and Noel Monahan at Windows during the 1990s.

Many poetry colleagues have graciously responded to the work in manuscript at various times, often making valuable suggestions. They include Nuala Ní Chonchúir and the Peers workshop, Todd Swift, Roger McGough, David Milligan-Croft, Shane Holohan, Kara Penn and others. Numerous friends have offered encouragement over the years. My appreciation to them all.

Thanks also to: Roger Gregg and his Bee-Loud Glade cabaret, who adapted and performed some of my poems in their shows at the Project Arts Centre and Smock Alley Theatre; Oran and Sarah at Seven Towers for welcoming me so often as a reader at their events; Mark Duff at the Base, who has recorded me performing many of my poems; and Vaughan Oliver and Marc Atkins for their fine book cover. Finally, love to my friends and family and above all, to Sara.

PATRICK CHAPMAN was born in 1968. He lives in Dublin. His poetry collections are *Jazztown* (Raven Arts Press, Dublin, 1991), *The New Pornography* (Salmon Poetry, Co. Clare, 1996), *Breaking Hearts and Traffic Lights* (Salmon, 2007), *A Shopping Mall on Mars* (BlazeVOX [Books], Buffalo, 2008) and *The Darwin Vampires* (Salmon, 2010). His collection of short stories is *The Wow Signal* (Bluechrome, UK, 2007).

Also a scriptwriter, he adapted his own published story for *Burning the Bed* (2003). Directed by Denis McArdle, this award-winning film starred Gina McKee and Aidan Gillen. He has written episodes of the BBC/RTÉ children's animated series *Garth & Bev* (Kavaleer, 2009); and a *Doctor Who* audio play, *Fear of the Daleks* (Big Finish, UK, 2007).

'The Orphan', from this collection, was a finalist in the third annual *Naugatuck River Review* Narrative Poetry Competition. Chapman was a finalist twice in the *Sunday Tribune* Hennessy Literary Awards. He won first prize for his story 'A Ghost' in the *Cinescape* Genre Literary Competition. In 2010 his work was nominated for a Pushcart Prize.